HUBBLE GARDENER

BISWAMIT DWIBEDY

Spuyten Duyvil
New York City

©2018 Biswamit Dwibedy
ISBN 978-1-947980-26-6
Cover Design: Yamini Reddy
Cover Art: FOLLOWING, 2017, Jesse Kanda

Library of Congress Cataloging-in-Publication Data

Names: Dwibedy, Biswamit, author.
Title: Hubble gardener / Biswamit Dwibedy.
Description: New York City : Spuyten Duyvil, [2018]
Identifiers: LCCN 2017057085 | ISBN 9781947980266
Classification: LCC PR9499.4.D915 A6 2018 | DDC 821/.92--dc23
LC record available at https://lccn.loc.gov/2017057085

CONTENTS

BODY: A MYTH	7
DINER	19
HUBBLE——THE MOVIE	35
EIRIK'S OCEAN	47
THIN KING	59
____ AND THE CITY	69
4 GIRLS, 3 BIRDS, 2 MEN	83
SEASHORE	93
GARDENER	105

BODY: A MYTH

                The year is
             soon to be our
           innocent center of
              what spans
             eras   see him
                get into
           a blue Minnesota
               twilight in
                    I
         A city spread like news
         gusts from an afternoon—
            an inward museum
                held by the
         birch and beech and elm

+

        the 3 of us +
a stone drinking milk
    written on secret
      unfurling Mississippi

          your hand on the edge
  under the table
     accidental touches
        recreating a scenario

experiments re: the infinite
productivity of language

brittle oral tradition
     over adjacent states

in Scandinavian accents

is a strand of the *shore*
      which means
   to witness a noise

was never found
   and is thus alive
& will go on giving

Alone

    because it captures
    a million colors as only
            you can see

        ancient children

they glow in the dark
they tease each other
with a nautical legend.

        It is said
when the ghost of an asp
is covered in ash it turns
into three red birds.

  One pleasures in the story of
  people who spread
a mastery over the moon.

  Another fled in return
   independent of the compass
to sing & even out the sea

  & powerful as many men
  a woman of striking wind.

Eirik the Red

Father of the first Finder of America
nurtured a vague little sense of religion

He pleasured in when you cannot see
wanderings and intermissions
of violence and kindness

incoherent after finding grapes

Prophetic North Star
Norse rose shape
glass hides honey, "milk
weed I touch   floats"

linger luckless, but act like a voyage

uncertainty & importance of
drift of sand or snow

impossible to dress an unity

Master's down in bed &
Wearing Icelandic

Sleep-state

Elsewhere all his life in
a city arranged on a violin.

I dreamt I couldn't regulate the crowds
coming in for eggs and coffee

sleep weighs down on us like mercury.

Inviting my body into folds of an apron

I go out walking to find the green
emits along their habit of
educating the eye.

Young stars I would like to paint
You confront, walking away from
the other side of the glass
seeing
also a non-entrance
a color within it
this morning
that lasts forever

and have a good time! A good time!

Masks

Two rooms in different parts of the city that look exactly alike
with no intention of a secret communication between
the ancient objects that house them.

From there you can see the skyline, approaching weather. The cinematic
snow of the word *we* once said in the singular.

And letting me show you, if you are sleeping next to me, my peacock mask.

We do not expect any information, but a part of the chat had survived
As memorabilia- family photographs,

Of people who have lost the same thing driving down that road.

And I tell him so every day. I tell him,
it's not my name until I act out what it means.

The sentence you never have flashes before your eyes.

He thinks you could conjure up the rain.

Someone should warn him, I act out
my falling as some bizarre optical illusion.

A possible hue it could have been
If I hadn't looked back

P(i)lot

I was beginning to feel like
I was
          the truth was
He had called it "a night"
for no reason   a field
an isolation upon which

like an heirloom; eyes
rising up to meet

The sky was concord.

Face against which forms the foreign
painting reportedly
an imprint on the silt

Distance placed in bones.

objects placed in language
to suggest spectrums.

On the surface of another river

one that exists along but never
the coast.
Can't be contained in itself
The outside I can't enter.

With the smile of an amnesiac
Who doesn't remember the heat

Alarm

uncharted and windy
enjoyment without margin
understood through disappointment
impressed to the morning air

my stanzaic water
turns on all sorts of
ulterior motives

exchanged for a lapse
in proximity

cold head buried in cooking

provisional limbs
trim the wick
the flame
crushed, corroding
intimacy

DINER

A.M.

    walking in
        —is
the noon today
a delay between
 arrivals
  & will not look
you in the eye
will not touch
the skin
 a con—

"fine" meant
in which
you can't tell
a fin
 from the net
 can't tell
what they want
 from their order

Arthur

        Our net of closeness and distance
        "in a ball of yarn" or fabric of
        fold by fold that unravels Arthur
         singing—your understanding

        It was a way of saying I want you
        also to have the same experience.

A lens through which we look at
touch where his lips had listed
possibilities awaiting at the door

 you wouldn't have recognised
 or even know that I was there

Rustle

always at hand yet impossible to touch
phrases that match the moment perfectly

continuity of the melodic line as a back
   ground emotion with twice the air

indulgent as a husband but not
faithful distance
        voice didn't fade into

a response to particulars was
                a rock carved
       desire accumulating delays
   between weather & refusal to speak
when he rudely shouts out what he wants
       & my life is not a personal thing-

          I think of us as friends
      but not so early in the morning

EGGS

Today's hunger used me like
instrumental syrup
a dozen eggs
strapped to your waist
the food was on
difficultly
difficulty
cultivated around us
smoke that
breaks this
inconsistent shade
invites
flotsam from a myth
a movie- thinking
winter would melt
under
"heat of moment"

Heat

Back in the heat of the kitchen
Our usual
arousals casually explained

a rush: when people come in
how he crudely "forms a fin;
a whole school" in the flipped
mirror of your eyes

moss made to look like a river
in wanderlust

       Can shimmer like
a sheen caught in the wind
craving a landscape

Splayed under the sun

says something to himself
Something else to the stove

I imagine you touching
depths in which
the sky doubles

Dear Sam

Attraction rubs off.
                You are
constantly touching the one I love.

Touches characteristic of a manuscript
 but not touches that indicate an author.

In an ancient book I read the body is considered
a meeting place of all the touches.

I depend on accidents while often touching
my own lips. These accidents I use
as a rule of thumb: whence and how they came

to be pleased and to please. My flesh beating
times suddenly still; confusions
the body can't remember; knowing that is simply
transitions on the screen

I said I but what I mean is my daughter, writer
sits and floats—"love is the grand use
one person rips of another"—

 between songs
 and dull parts of the afternoon

would be seen coming out of his house.

Body

(for Rosmarie Waldrop)

The voice opens to the body
but the body cannot keep the voice

I thought it were otherwise

my hopes were crushed by this knowledge

Outside, a crowd unbuttoned
               into exclamations
                             exposed himself
                    glittering
     on a spider-web

"all this is in the present
& in the mirror, every night

possibilities predicting
a tongue caught in
grain of sentences

I had badly wanted a story of my own

Not a body but a form
without boundary or edge

Voice

    contained in the trivial
something ancient, with no intention

        a voice can cling to you
       in the middle of a sentence
    & pacing back and forth
           your window, weather
acknowledged as an accomplice.

Their eyes had seen differently
          creating a path now
for the moon just beginning to come up in
      these books I have called my home
         & morning somewhere else

       I hear his voice takes
      where a wing would form

        In another myth
he'd have swallowed the sun.

        His horoscope said it would taste like
      any other fruit, when I thought
        it was more like an egg
      he was about to crack.

Rush

Our acts are mistakes
but nobody tells you
regulars regulate joy
 in what one does
thrive in the lack of

touching repeatedly
calls out my name
or curse I mishear

 the noise drenched
already in someone
else's attention.

      A stir
   under the rush
   an eye on each
           fingers' spiral

     hands on fire—
   crowds collecting
   clouds the color of

        sweat—
       screaming
    I love my job!

Fur

Your eggs are lovely Hubble

Unfurling at what speed are
moving away from one another

He knows good food arouses & inspires
& anything sung is always in the present tense.

Driving by, we saw signs of ruined nations
& dreams in which you resembled an animal
had found extreme comfort in the plush hide

Carnage of my collaborative seductions

noon again
o blinding
   lane/law/n
                  America is unreal
                  a sound you ride on
                  turning the air green.

 And gather, hidden, on a window: a grassy gown:
this notion of a home you would have laughed at.

Swollen red river, moves along the corner of
strike and it's electric

       incapable geometry.

An airy place unique to each artery
—this is that.   This was that
which emits at night.   Clear as Vodka &
oiling down the wind with your two names.

To the coming together of their meaning in a sentence
are a river falling over. Incomprehensible men
Will crush it up in a rage

and tied to his wrist
bones floating in the sound

       I said the road destroys me
but going away I will take an inventory

Skin

what wills unfold
gilded on a glacier

in utterances common and untrue
the news is a déjà vu

Glass orchestrating a long division

I saw him get into a blue van

I think the eyes are a museum

of salt drying on lashes as slept
& I serve underneath when he
sails in & wets his beak in my
stream of
lover of

"single men and their single meals"

Cheering the team into an embrace
abridged into a single week's
reversal of my desire for
another skin growing on
this morning
it's a mistake he says
that holds the bridges together.

And if you remember it extends
through watery flowers of unique self
cutting into borders

A scene in which our city is flooded

& I leave you with your many friends

HUBBLE—
THE MOVIE

Screen

I believe this is something you said
"hopelessly confused by time".

We watch a crack become a spun thing
as a forest begins to stroke the sky.

As a separate form of cinema
we cannot quibble with the screen

within the face, the many faceted
raising an ocean you haven't heard of.

I thought the many strands were an accomplice
organized as a mosaic.

 The problem is the end of
 love & biology, an alliance, a single
mote of our encounter.

like glass gave an insight

but nothing caught a reflection.

SEEN

Benign night had led to a foreign place

Had let the scenery disperse in their eyes
as constellations I read forth.

      "Burn me something else"
he said (and) I was afraid
of the moon becoming a laughing matter

The horoscope, a script I used to align
his experience to mine.

But he would not have understood.

He went on explaining instead an incidental light

A line that appeared when a spark fell

documenting the details of our conversation

Scene

Through the thin fabric I could see
the skin's becoming miles
away from your cheek--

was only a trick on the eye

      Friends become landscapes +

      was nodding off at a bar when
      I begged him to recognize

what one calls fictionalizing

who went to console the inconsolable sisters

Conversations one must apologize for in writing

we've declined the surprise by filling in the gaps

At the Movie

I thought if I could project memories onto the screen
it would help me retain an image in my mind later, color
accumulating, sculptural

—as a corollary, a group of neurons form
a miniature world—mouths facing each other
whose firing breaks a chain

The many separate photons of a laser beam are so entangled
that it is as if there is just one photon in the beam—
but to see one has moved, there must be activity somewhere
symbolizing a change of particulars

—a room in which you could hear "consciousness" at work—

If everything in nature is an inherent "consciousness-ability", then
human beings have access to information about weather whenever

Borders

snowflakes streak the vast while
I am against you
like a skyline

& found what moves patterns empathetic viewpoints

                established in repeating

a surface that curves smoothly to partly occlude itself

On the borders—on-screen as in any cell of an eye

        —emerging from an ocean—

can organize a state-space—a space of all possibilities

 in network activation

—maps—the color of dusk—

—rush of smoothness—assuming—

if a surface is smooth
so is the image producing it

After Noon

light of recognition
reflected aimlessly
his body along
will hover.

As now you will
say: Can I?
Repeating
Let Me. Be Mine.
And the Many
in the forest turn concrete. Your breath
a staggering plateau. The delicate marriage
of bones.

An oar unraveled
Whatever rippled
roughly shaped like
another orbit

similarities we must reclaim.

An I on the other side
the other hand, awakens
architecture. like mica
inside the eyes.

 Wheat, dirt
elongated seasons.

That move, so assured.

   The sky multiplied within each vein. Your tender body
in a blur. Now snow. Like glaciers in motion. To say,
    it's gravitational. Or subterranean heart will unwind the sea.
To say: a brother, unformed, lives on, in green underwater
of my home. Of stones. In neat pieces come undone.

Telegram

An architecture elongated along each vein now turns
    delicate forest inside your body turns speechless and
        unrecognizable which is beautiful and autonomous
           like a sun spun of white threads and slivered
              weather you can touch, taste, and it moves you'll note
              through the night   to your wrist   in lighted vaults

a glass face and my pulse, chaotic, telegrams
escaping orbits: distant friend; bird, now tongue
inside fire, folded, it is summer, it is a flying I
   watched you curve so gracefully
                  into your name
           of impenetrable water
                      will not be photographed
                            will calmly drown

EIRIK'S OCEAN

Year Unknown

Little Cousins-

        The weather is very cold here. We the students of the white throne
have never seen anything like it. We thought we were home but it is difficult
to not be fictitious in so far and fair a place. Sometimes a letter says
you will see me someday but what I send
is always badly aimed
and we miss that fine edge. We love the black buzz of the marrow
too homogeneously. Our sacred neighbors are angered by the noise
but still send their sympathy, insisting I live always drowning
the pronoun, a faded flower, the difference between a letter
and a poem: a little book in the grass. I go out walking and find
the green emits along their eyes &
going against the appearance of my lover. Leave my kisses,
a faint note in pencil. The wilderness about my breath,
Called Back—
The Dead need a boat to carry their grave wealth.
Make them know I love them, though our alliances
are losing foothold, and to trace them would be a huge burden.

READ

One book says "eider" and the other "bird"

And said she likes how it sounds different each time.

Two versions derived from a red dress & his red beard

sought redress. Under a glacier named White Shift

Two ghosts derived from the year 985 or 986. 25 set sail

Count the 9 that didn't get married. A wealthy girl

Deep-mined daughter of eastward brightness at night

drawing on information from within her won family

some fates remain as left out as described

4 girls, 3 birds, 2 men and 1 stone believed in

unbelievable things lit up   inside the ice

a green compiled by his own son.

The Red

                                                          Diplomat and diarist notes,
Never had I seen people of such reddish color   Dear Sir

              you are a name shared by every tongue

                        but nothing catches a reflection.

                              They painted clouds instead to depict
        what friends tell you about your life
                and you think is a prison. A prism

                          not a distinct direction the light scatters in

              the waves come in from the inside

                                    It's a gorgeous view, he said
                            he's beautiful as an animal
                trapped in the wind—
                      a boy
                      by the museum
                      for contemplation
                                    each movement
                                      a fold of time

                            I thought the book was a war
                                  in the middle
                                  of which we
                                  just run
                                  out of lives

Reed

said I shouldn't name

   dead silent centuries

light on an insomnia

a sound I count on

each finger denies

   surface experience

I mine by

telling no one

                                                                         burnt corners of

                                                                          icebergs touching

                                                                            rake, reed, stem

                                                                         changed hands

                                                                      two landscapes in

                                                                     memory followed by

                                                                     one voice without

White Shift

    We have no map he claimed
    according to the crystal sea
    nothing turned green in
    one version of the legend
    both of them promising
    young men but Eirik

wouldn't give up his faith

      raven and wolf are
impersonal in place I
   would have gone in
     or at least a little closer

      to the wind a chest
        of gold children
           with red hands

they're punished for having hidden
    travellers counted into an ideal couple
        who couldn't recall having seen its like

Manuscript

and there sighted unknown lands
at the mercy of contrary winds
wild grapes are grown here as
a way of counting longitude

860 names ornament a part
of the world called undiscovered

gods go on wearing diamond
wind arrived at a historian's
ambition marked by removes

Red-Shift

glow in the dark helm of

awe on your arms I sa

  id like it here can I

repeat enough times

just above your wings

encircling orbits adjust

history weighs warriors

Open

        Turning the light on
        the blue bodied boy
        does he know how
        to resist each morning
        2 summers we are
        riddled seers of

a restless sail and his memory
 just stops by your hand

reaching for the day's mysteries.

        Now it was time to think of coffee.

or syllables one must contemplate

      when he calls out
a question you mishear

  that is not what they want

We don't call that noise but
kingdom opposed to other things

MOVIE

 lengthening shadows
sacred nights cultivate in
the vicinity of I don't know
how a boy could take the sun
in his mouth the most aquatic
novel's main theme is renewal

why one body falls and another
doesn't see him perched in it *is*
silently coming down again
        I think
in the forest means a tribe
dwelling will reconstruct
lovely Hubble , Edwin

this memory   seems strange
step by stone who gathered
the sea into mild tremors
sky enclosed as if in a letter
    by your memory I have
known more of you

THIN KING

A thing occurring within the skin, she said, there was too much intensity
going on there. But when we got there, there was no there
                                                                                                    there
in the new sports arena, an episode is recalled as
                            games people play
"*innings I'd turn to pure lyric*"
                                  in an architectural setting
a parallel universe.
                      Said my walls need to be stripped
of this ancient monument
                which took years to build
and then they each lost a thumb, a son the
next door would open and there you would be,
ready to go on a vacation.

              There's a boy who's a Krishna

And he thinks you will recognize this song.

You've never claimed to touch those worlds, but they only take up existence in the sound of your name. It's a specific kind of life. And you are not in it The colors are recognizable and the shapes you'd like, though that seems contrived. I'd rather see signs of you arriving at these constellations surprised names await. In the pencil—a possibility—erased last night. A pause decorated by your absence. I used it away as numerous pages—
on the touch of your hand I love very much, but only from afar.

Body II

An attention to details can explain away these senses.
Then a mirror clears the air.

of unknown uniform behavior, I was never scared of
stormy weather as a boy.
                                    Because the salt
of your sweat is related to the restless
and sleepless, you see

no other neighborhood will be made of such good friends

Or no one else walking into a bar
would flood the empty selves that sharpen
you are convinced
your chances of just running into him there
restless in the many greens
—an animal
thinking— I'm a hunter—
I should listen.

Book 1

One day I found a book buried deep in the ground,   and to my surprise I really liked
your fine fingers of indifference. Oh, I don't know- maybe there is a private language
a love that dare not speak it's a rowing on waters too delicate to taste   as an oar

A fin reflecting on the sky, susceptible to misinterpretation

Photographs often taken for a pleasure in the blueprint

Like the sound of paper ruffling everywhere.

I like how you had actually fallen but
on-screen it's the light that moves my thoughts
whereas the pages stay untouched
thick against the fabric

2

       I'm trying to reason why it is a photograph I look at everyday

Said she could hear me through the night, but I'm worried
it's already morning   & I
     start collecting quotes, collaging notes, like a colorist
     could make the two eggs hatch   in a new light

     It was the sun in your mouth,
your hand burning
on the snow that never melts

I thought there were crystal trees lit by an interior sun
but the moon takes precedence.

It changes every face photographed into a view
you always sat with your back to.

A long history of absence dissolved in a touch
and I lay there thinking, it was brave
I was awake.

Erased by what I see
on the thin shell of a boundary

Like wings of certain insects

Silken as the tune's image
Sink drop by drop
punched into the margin

Naked, the film's thin weight
Can't take the blame
of invention
to keep repeating

a line, its direction
getting lost again and again

But when will its notes connect
to reinvent
the scenario of that seduction—

Gestures of a dance so small
they are a waste of the radio.

And not unlike particles on a sensitive screen

Your presence thrives in a soft Braille, but it is disconcerting to think
shards of brightness must constantly erupt into flesh for it to matter

 Under such waters
             & on the tongue of a surge
an increased displacement of the object
produces a greater appearance of color.

You seek: the crest as a test of perceptions,
layers of distortions
as mist. You detail the ambiguity of its depths,
with echoes

__ AND THE CITY

___AND THE CITY

Walking creates a frame—
one pause modeled after another
till it is a bridge over the river
that cuts across your body.

light crossing the water
replaced the leaves

Some film found there
as events existing

vein after vein, grids
of information
scratched out
the eyes

The perceived sizes of the moon in its move last night
    were taken as evidence of the bird's flight

                                Owing to their likeness to one another
            they break into two small arcs

                        On the surface of the moon, it's two small scars
eyeing an imaginary satellite.

                        He said, "saved by the book"
but what he reads are inaccurate visual information
                we have settled for.

A novel of thank you   not to be told at all
and certainly not as well told. Not as well told.

                        *

I want to hear him through the night. The skin in its noon at night,
 how there are many moons. But they don't melt into a bank because
  glaciers rooted in the planet can become flotillas along our world, but not in it.

It might have begun as a vague sense of a distance, but it's luminous
by the time you arrive   white trim on a wave

what city isn't in conflict?

*

The background, a feat of balance, a bone broken into wings

A shaky signature etched into the camera.

The distorted nudity he slips on

a recognition
grooved by your hand

A payment not an exchange.

A rejection of the visual idea to execute an intellectual one.

I'm still married, says the Bachelor.

His hardness released as a hinge.

Barter

Or perhaps two modes of thinking have crossed, creating the potential for an event
Sentences are miniatures in which situations are contained

A kiss you never felt was the salt of my mouth

                             is how she kept track
                             of music inside a lark
                             in reference to

               leaves with eyes
               anticipating
               an accidental photograph

A loaf of rain above my farm is an enormous ash, sheaf
based on what happened   over and over
an experience or emotion so aptly called your name

PLOVER

     This doesn't correspond to something in the outside world
            but
Sifting through facts and things looking back
          at you
roams a dialogue
     between two discords.

as if such strokes were only missing . A hand that can
    make this a face abandoned under the skin
& traveling in numerous directions
forms a ring
  arranged as a profile
     can be heard
       by speaking into the old ruin

which is alive somewhere else as the basis of such doubling

As news stifled by the ones who wait

But with the tide, new patterns would unfold

characteristics of the shore other dependent entirely on the plover

Film

Quotes, others, mine, times in which
I use them to describe what no one saw

as they often seem hidden by a web
       where the ideal is parallel

I would have drawn you accurately.

I was only writing to keep up with regulars
that regulate joy in poems I recognize
bewilderment and astonishment were sisters
as they read each other's work

Bream

As a boy, even before he knew how to read,
he wrote a book that would turn you blind.

I dreamt we were a part of his message,
the reading of a bream he touched

which no sheaf could recollect

weeds and stones the water employed
before evening turns into a sequence,
a riverbed

which at minimal intensity is a single pulse

becomes dust   of your absence

I love the letters m & o, the r laid into a vacancy.

Now we steal quotations and pad out poems.

If it is desire turning the timing of an event into a series
of delays
then isn't desire for an event also the desire of a delay?

                quiet water
                milked into
                a grammar
                                  as if maps
often pattern how moisture rising to the skin can process

the first map was of ephemera, streams

the surface was flawless till someone's seeing slit it

plagued by its course, it shrinks,

inside a grain of sand, a desire

to belong to the dead.
                    We are being read
by those who have no eyes. Gestures float

on your palms, patterns
the past follows
to protect us.

So why hide?

Bridge

Inventor of allusive shadows and promising letters,
out on your walk steps and stones are
states I call my present tending
the remainder we have termed syntax.

You cut my voice. Vein after vein—you turn to
ward your own body, a question mark, still

shrinking   a curve, a code
one step—and a foreign world appears

OPERETTA

Here buried an operetta
as our being together

brought out by chance

On a complicated dawn
chromatic values that enter
a room that is like a dream

The first recognizable patterns
were fingerprints

Difficulty of a foreign language
misplaced in a love for

Impossibility, construe a film
and so we began to chart

the body rowed away in haste
a science of resisting sleep.

Assigning each star
to a new constellation

4 GIRLS,
3 BIRDS,
2 MEN

Bird One

The bird draws its voice from the land

and its flight marked streams, canals, marshes

"any photographer will tell you the same"

A book can compress and release time

floating into a present and there I was,

she said, "the novel is basically a creation

that releases what is essential" —which

doesn't correspond to a deep north or south of

"I'm rotting here"—the artist explained

"these are wings —these are songs —these are

birds that measure time differently

and as a suspension of the difference

—they replace one other.

Bird Two

Stands on fringes of this day and decides
to where the new voyage might be.

The worn hand, a map

written on water and I thought
               I saw
that glittering, a semblance.

An accident can look like you were trying
               to align

There is someone here who trespasses

where I was. Or are you just
an aftertaste; a mistake the tongue could make?

bits of a song, meanings from different names
spread into a purple called your body.

He knows each color was conspiring to see
Our hands forge a likeness. A paltry resonance
once called laughter.
               A storm caught inside a book

patterns you cannot distinguish from
the ropes and ribbons it makes of you.

Bird Three

Both thunderbolt and diamond, my friend
gently helped by the sway of
spread along to other parts
symbolizing the union of compassion and
the dark and obscure
wringing his hands over a map of the world, thinking
              the obvious analogy is with water,
& the earliest examples of writing
found in ruined cities
that line along
the now dead riverbed.

660 or 661

Dear Cousin

I bring you a Fern from my own Forest, where I play every day:
It is August 1876. She writes "Loved and little Sister—
we call her the "minute hand." And when thought wavers,
it cannot be said that it is not certainly to test the sentence

during Eirik's days. He had a shorthanded sickle and an iron blade
and even those were scarce. Eirik or his blacksmith
would heat up, purify it further

at the trace of a fingertip
three strands of a thread

drawn at the mouth of the Swan,
an island so fertile
you would have had to call it green.

The duck population is lower now.

Mother is timid for you, remembering
dark mystical tradition .

A community taken up by truth
excluded allure of
noise that is infinite
in which you trace specifics

of infinity, by itself
to infinity, by itself

Saint

Through the thin fabric I could see it doesn't mean a piece of cloth but
                          secret and fictional I
                                proved unpopular and discarded.

Migration followed a similar pattern
                a journey forever forward to a home that never was
                    pushed out by unfavorable weather
                            and attracted to promise of new land
                                      named after a patron saint

He had hands that changed color as we worked,

        And everything he touched turned an attribute
of this immaterial world

Twin

                                        devoted to another man
                                    as dear as a brother
                                        so how to count
                                    when he comes at
                                    unpredictable hours
                                        incarnate in the
                                      sacred endearment

        some relic snatched
and then returned.

Carrying entire landscapes in one hand

and assuming the sun to be a ripe mango
body raised to orbit around   pleasure
                                    was the fee.

        Captivating accent,
doesn't enter your mouth but flies across
a mild curse
        under which a wave
is a drop of sweat in the ocean

Wander

tearing open
to expose endless
streets turn
rumor into news

record called "scrap"
or "greatest" or
who dance to forget

came out of the water
dripping honey

wondered at messages
brings
the wanderer's end

born to the wrong name

saying which
might result in
that didn't happen

Spine

Someone else's experience of another winter, a horizon
made out of an eye in love with gravity
rolls in on waves and waits
there to sculpt the air
naming things that never returned

I felt your gaze along my spine & looked back
to affirm   the evidence
                          a saint
was wrongly alleged to believe
the body was beyond
lines each palm would unfold

Trees align into a green that heals   the eye
he carried in his pocket   turned ice.

believed the next winter would be milder
         and moved further north

In search of two meanings of the word
their difference defy the distance from
a home around your neck
wearing the season's new color

SEASHORE

CARL

Our system of the great diffuse
could be used
as a metaphor on the sundial
but could never belong to any language

And since it is hard to deceive relationships between
limits of the sky and absolute brightness

Exemplary Midwestern charm
Translated from   a strand
                                  I weave
                           to save thread
I must have misread: seashores
were the inspiration behind a science of speech

and a prominent American scientist believed

entire galaxies get caught in
a sense of intention in each silence
at the table

lost in a musical memory

Wick

                        Both particle and wave
the first spark is a stone
that burns to this day
with 108 names
       & without a messenger
kept falling forth
       of constant speed
with respect to all things that curve
are revered will
never come to an end

As a moon along its own earth
and everything we look at
is a lamp   a map, recalled

as much sun as our distance from
decided upon a new home

       relying heavily on a fertile wind

& as a part of a stellar arrangement

years of little movement
became a thin ring around the wick

Yolk

Growth rings surround the circumference of
        Birch in snow
                show
a strong climactic shifting

foreshadowed by letters   (seasons grow over our eyes)
                      (and translating through the skies)

The first American to discover an expanding egg

Based on unbelievable observational evidence

patterned in parts to correspond to reality

which echoed speculations about
the light that has been unable still
to find there's a future we will

proportional to our distance from one +
one equals the limits of my thought

said—secrets of the sky were essentially a photographic problem
They aren't phenomenon bound by their own appearance.

Honey

Not necessarily a continuation, but not a new beginning either, its as if
his friends don't consider the messy details of neuroscience,
against the background of which the sentence
(what I'm supposed to say) is misunderstood.

Between the weather and length of all moonlight

whatever mistaken for the truth
just slightly beyond my reach

sound I marked for your arrival

that timely knowledge of no trace

but salt that lines these ships
mapped on a film of grease.

Golden shards floating
in the honeyed   I'd
Leave it on the table and walk quietly back

To your instructional tonic
to the parched &
perched between position and stance.

Each stranger
as an assurance
remains the news.

Shell

The body is evidence. Of patterns that entwine
and something invisible to our eyes can survive
our knowing a naming need not interfere
with what is between me and the delay to understand

To continue as a sequence.

                I saw him involved in a strange sleep.

My staring at some parts of the film for a natural increase of
strands that change each scene.

They're in a new locale; singing in a language I don't understand.

It's a dream-sequence. Moving through the fog
in precisely choreographed steps

I sift through the scene till I see
crowds that refuse to share our love for a song
because to them, each step is effeminate; a shadow
of the presence we are too joyous to contradict.

And a wild fire caught under the influence
of improbable desires, as doting friends await

to connect empty glasses to their drinkers, who are too ecstatic
to remember white curtains swell anyways, oozing out of the seam
snow that covered the thin screen

and how I slip on the ice
is how the ringed horizon spiralizes in you: with disdain
for the classical design called proportions of the body.

Let me touch the axis.

Truth has no confines but a lower layer I'd strike
if the sun strikes the mirror in
which his friends broke
with his jokes   In laughing
a person is bejeweled
breaking eggshells

STAY, SEE—

I thought the leaves at this window of mine
Were a bit of the sky wearing green.
you tread to remember nervous patterns
but I've stopped saving the design

 when the pollen floats
        I stopped in the middle of
                if the lights are on
you have gone to bed
and will not wake up

      (this on New Year's Eve)

names accrue a map of uses for the
                star-shaped
  traced in flowers   beheld the world
          in closed eyes
              a fissure thinking
      it's a vessel of
            rice and wheat
spread out in all directions.

measured in finest line-work
              along his hands
never asked me for water
but clenched, a fruit
        and the world blurred
the distance between our homelands

The season's first prolific dust

Now this ash all over your house

Did you travel far enough?

Moving away from __ she said

"books are all we have left" of

those times don't correspond to

an inside but the very many stars

form a surface of __ under which

patterns rot +

the birds are drunk again

GARDENER

Unknown

Ancient lake and trace unknown
A feather could follow you home—
A flake of snow, distinct and lost

projecting the self into action
from barbarism to civilization
A small short-lived settlement
promised growth

A saint with short bloody reigns
feels at images of an island

for all our mistakes
had actually started a landslide

"I'm burning"—the child said,
and nearby, on one hand, stood
that which betrayed our trust

Dear Body—Bird,

A letter always feels to me like autumn
across the shape of your eyes
and in the center of desire—a quotation.

Lovely alien floating in the throat.

A lily found there.
Passing from personas to portraits,
pleats presented in the throat
Though I am to recollect
the arm reaching for.

Birds amend homewards in stern pleasure.
I wish they would tarry the frost
I wish the delay were kinder, a precious inn
painting years we shall journey when you come home again.

As a proof of recognition
The road is faithful. Vegetation continues along it
like yellow paper—the purest of all regions in the garment of life.

Its beauty relates your eyes to the moon during an afternoon,
A silver on the windless mystery
and in the back of my throat
mechanisms that disappear into a language
I do not speak

And mourn that loss in a foreign tongue.

It's snowing here again. Green divided by white.
Thank the dear little storm calmly detaining me in
between a remainder and as the evidence indicates,
a little world of sisters

Pages

Wander and return
grief for grief
pagan pages
sailing in fleets.

Winged young boys
glittering over
fields and fields of
now covered path
turned murderous.

Of where and when they met
connecting resources
redistributing the news.

Men go roving over
the mouth of the river
whose shield is thunder.

I look at you and a wonder
takes me weaving a fine mind.
The sea too close kin for
our story takes such strange turns.

Massacred children and forgetting queens
The king is drinking with his diplomats &
scattered unmistakable characteristics
across whitecaps or nightcaps.

RECURRENCE OF NOMADIC CONDITIONS

the water takes on a human voice
indeterminate directions it sparks
measured into paper cuts what is
    the ancient to you Sir?

      of indifferent worlds

and submarine behavior a sailor
sings to icicles around his breath

      unpredictable weather
we've treated the dead like a king
    or vice-versa

two versions of claiming ancestors
but we couldn't have measured
the distance within them doubling
we go back to saving daylight

The past coming true at a staggering speed

        returning free from snow
        now the sun, a disaster
           The year 1000 was one in
           which they were not content
           with fixed horizons

           the fragrant grass
        breathing in slopes when
              centuries await ahead.

        They've decided to winter there.
        They've discussed amongst themselves
           what country it might be

               but before he could answer
they sighted a glacier

               And everywhere birds
        wherever there was water.

               In a sea I put to sleep
whose hard home is knowledge
his for the taking, but he takes time.

Edwind

        It is he who discovered the olive
     Not a replica on display
          Strangers caught saying you are the opposite of
    The body wrongly affected by the mouth

  The light swerves out of his shirt and
    my body grows to the left

       He sees it as a face

  Let me touch your lips.

      They are mine

  No need to feel duped—it is a play
  on the word
  "body"—a pause
  or delay
  I wait out
what word isn't

the name of a
   seeking

Islands

We see the sea reaching precisely
for the subject is a shipman's card

I suggest you write on it in red.

In the welcoming light the dead
have shed their skin & become
 more than I see when what I cannot see is-
-lands to which they have lent their names

                                            Must have been a life more fully lived than
                                            Here add an I to his sons of unreturned

                                            men sentenced to sea realized they were
                                            Farther inland. Some were driven back

                                            And some explored the landscape there.

3 MEN—ALONE—AT A BAR

I want to steal
            years abridged
into a wick   we are
always inside an enraged line

waiting

a pencil raised to the full moon.

But it wasn't you coming down
I caught
drying on his lashes as
they speak to me of my absence

the salt
a stain
on the seam
one should
contemplate the syllable.

Because I loved the mysterious
we lived on alms, misplaced &
what anybody else will not want.

We hear a mesh of wires, sensitive to touch
and color of his shirt
arranged on a violin
becomes volume
across oceans

I see him looking at lines of light on water
and directions double
the rupture   a key to the read.

I said the color of his shirt but what I mean
is stance. Your friend did something to tell me
how I shouldn't hope for that or maybe
I've confused the polite twice today.

But going back to that night   I never thought of fighting with my friends
           as a pastime
& do not regret spending so much   on each episode & yes

It was a stranger who first called me that. My name is
Something picked up at an airport.
And it really did happen this way
She said—   "call me whatever you want" or—
she likes how it sounds different each time
or
why were you calling me that?

I could feel what he thought of himself
and likewise, I'm sure, he experienced
A hook.
            To conjure up the rain
As in a song
     in a corner you turn
          all that green
I count (for a friend)
    an ear   to the wind

who forgot
who fought   as they must

make sure you win

ACKNOWLEDGMENTS

Poems from this collection were published by HarperCollins India in 2017 as *Ancient Guest*. The author would like to thank the publishers for their support.

Poems from this collection also appeared as a chapbook called *Eirik's Ocean*, published by Portable Press/Yo-Yo Labs in 2016.

Some poems from this collection have also been in 1913 Journal. The author would like to thank the editors for their support over the years.

These poems owe a great debt to the work of Leslie Scalapino, Mei-mei Berssenbrugge, Norma Cole, Laura Moriarty, Fanny Howe, Ann Lauterbach, Stacy Doris, Rosmarie Waldrop, Susan Howe, and, most importantly, Sandra Doller and Cole Swensen. I am grateful for their support, work, and words.

Much thanks to Yamini Reddy and Nishi Banka for their efforts on the cover, and to Jesse Kanda, for allowing me to use his work.

www.ingramcontent.com/pod-product-compliance
Lightning Source LLC
Chambersburg PA
CBHW081752100526
44592CB00015B/2391